THE LEGACY OF ELIZEBETH SMITH FRIEDMAN

The Extraordinary Life and Achievements of the Pioneering Code Breaker, Astonishing Poet and Mother of Cryptology

By

Ruby A. Myers

TABLE OF CONTENT

A Fascinating account of the American Cryptanalyst and Author who decrypted enemy codes in both World Wars and solved smuggling cases in the Prohibition Era.

Elizebeth Smith Friedman (1892–1980) was an innovative American codebreaker and cryptanalyst. She played a crucial role in deciphering a wide range of intricate codes and ciphers from the early to mid-20th century. Elizebeth's journey began at Riverbank Laboratories, where she unraveled enigmatic meanings concealed within Shakespeare's writings. Later, she formed a formidable alliance with her equally esteemed spouse who was known as the father of the National Security Agency, William Friedman. Elizebeth's story is characterized by her exceptional intelligence, unwavering resolve, and unwavering fortitude. Collectively, they confronted the obstacles presented by World War I, unraveling intricate codes that determined the destiny of entire nations.

During the era of Prohibition in the United States, Elizebeth shifted her focus to the realm of organized crime, deciphering encrypted messages that protected the illicit activities of the underground economy and ensuring that the principles of fairness and justice were upheld. She displayed exceptional intelligence and made significant contributions during World War II by deciphering the enigmatic messages of Axis spies working in South America.

Elizebeth Smith Friedman made notable accomplishments in an area that was traditionally male-dominated. Her work not only significantly influenced national security, but also served as a catalyst for the advancement of women in the field of cryptanalysis and codebreaking for future generations.

CHAPTER ONE

Ultra and The Enigma Machine

Ultra refers to an intelligence initiative conducted by the Allies. Ultra was an Allied intelligence initiative that successfully intercepted and deciphered highly secure communications from the German, Italian, and Japanese armed forces. This significant achievement played a crucial role in the ultimate triumph of the Allies during World War II. At Bletchley Park, a British government facility situated north of London, a select group of code breakers devised methods to decipher encoded messages intercepted from German operators. The messages were encrypted using electrical cipher machines, with the most significant ones being the Enigma and, later in the war, the advanced Tunny machine. Bletchley Park's production of top-tier military intelligence was designated as Ultra.

On a daily basis, the German military transmitted several encrypted messages, encompassing a wide range of content, including directives endorsed by Adolf Hitler, comprehensive reports on the situation made by frontline generals, as well as weather updates and inventory of supply ships. A significant portion of this material was acquired by the Allied forces, frequently within a few hours of its transmission. The decrypted messages, known as "raw decrypts," were seldom taken out of Bletchley Park. However, analysts at that location examined the decrypted material and created intelligence reports that deliberately hid the actual origin of the data.

The Enigma machine was employed by the Germans to encrypt their military communications throughout World War II. The Enigma machine, a device that integrated electrical and mechanical elements, originated from various designs that were proposed for patent as early as 1918 in Germany and were subsequently manufactured for commercial use starting in the early 1920s. Resembling a typewriter in appearance, the device was operated by batteries and possessed exceptional portability. Besides a keyboard, the device was equipped with a lamp board that featured 26 stenciled letters, each illuminated by a miniature lightbulb positioned behind them. A cipher clerk entered a message in plain German on the keyboard, causing the letters to be sequentially lighted on the lamp board. The helper manually transcribed the letters to create the encoded message, which was subsequently transmitted via Morse Code.

The lamp board was designed such that each bulb was linked to a specific letter on the keyboard through an electrical connection. However, the wiring was routed through a series of rotating wheels, causing the connections to constantly change as the wheels rotated. Typing the same letter on the keyboard would result in a sequence of varying letters on the lamp board. The constantly shifting network of connections is what made Enigma exceptionally difficult to decipher.

The initial triumph over the German military Enigma was achieved by the Polish Cipher Bureau. During the winter of 1932–33, the Polish mathematician Marian Rejewski successfully inferred the wire arrangement within the three moving wheels of the Enigma machine. Rejewski obtained assistance from the French secret service in the form of pictures depicting pages from an Enigma operating handbook for the months of September and October 1932. Prior to commencing the encryption process, an Enigma operator would adjust the three wheels of the Enigma machine (four in the case of variants utilized by the German naval) to different initial settings that were likewise familiar to the intended recipient. Rejewski achieved a significant advancement by devising a technique to determine the initial positions of the wheels in each intercepted German transmission. As a result, Poland successfully deciphered encrypted German signals from 1933 to 1939.

During the summer of 1939, Poland sent comprehensive intelligence, including details about Rejewski's bomba, a machine he invented in 1938 to decrypt Enigma messages, to Britain and

France. In May 1940, a significant modification was made to the Enigma system, which effectively closed the vulnerability that Rejewski had previously exploited to determine the initial positions of the wheels. The implementation of novel techniques at Bletchley Park in 1940 facilitated the ongoing decryption of German air force and army communications by code breakers. Nevertheless, German naval signals, particularly the crucial communication to and from U-boats in the North Atlantic, remained concealed.

CHAPTER TWO

Wild Bill

William J. Donovan was renowned for his propensity for expeditiousness. He was an American attorney, military officer, and diplomat who supervised (1942–45) the U.S. Office of Strategic Services (OSS) during World War II. Donovan commenced his legal career in Buffalo in 1907. In 1916, he enlisted in the New York National Guard and was stationed on the Mexican border. During World War I, he served in France as a member of the 165th Infantry Regiment, which was previously known as the renowned New York 69th Regiment. He achieved the rank of colonel and received the Congressional Medal of Honor. In 1922, he was designated as the United States district attorney for the western region of New York. From 1924 to 1929, he held the position of assistant attorney general in the Justice Department.

In the 1930s, he resumed his legal profession while also sustaining his political affiliations both domestically and internationally. In 1940-41, President Franklin D. Roosevelt requested Donovan to develop proposals for establishing a centralized intelligence agency for the United States. Donovan was designated coordinator of information on July 11, 1941. He was appointed as the head of the recently established OSS on June 13, 1942. This military agency was tasked with gathering foreign intelligence and executing counterpropaganda and covert action missions. It conducted operations worldwide, excluding Latin America and Gen. Douglas MacArthur's Pacific command, and was particularly active in Europe. Donovan was promoted to the rank of brigadier general in 1943. Despite being a prominent supporter of establishing a central intelligence organization during peacetime, he chose not to participate in the newly formed Central Intelligence Agency (CIA) in 1947. In the years 1953-1954, he held the position of United States ambassador to Thailand.

In November 1941, President Franklin D. Roosevelt designated "Wild Bill" as the Coordinator of Information (COI). In this role, "Wild Bill" urgently requested the establishment of a cryptography unit to be developed from the beginning. He approached a woman who was gaining recognition as the prominent figure in the field of cryptology. Elizebeth Smith Friedman, an accomplished codebreaker, had already made significant contributions to cryptographic operations for the U.S. War Department in World War I. She also played a crucial role in decoding numerous messages exchanged by rumrunners during Prohibition. Furthermore, she served as a key witness in the prosecution of the world's most influential international narcotics smuggling syndicate. Additionally, she held the distinction of being the first female codebreaker for both the Treasury Department and the Coast Guard.

CHAPTER THREE

Elizebeth Smith's Early Life and Career

In the late 1930s, Friedman and her team became the pioneering American organization to acquire knowledge of Germany's Enigma machine. As a result of their endeavors, the Coast Guard provided crucial intelligence to the U.S. Army, Navy, and State Department. She successfully deciphered 4,000 codes that played a crucial role in dismantling a fascist espionage network in South America. Her achievements garnered significant attention from the media, leading to her being prominently featured in lots of famous magazines. The media consistently highlighted the "astonishing" aptitude of a lady to decipher intricate texts. In addition, she possessed the talents of a poet, and had expertise in both Shakespearean literature and Mayan archeology. Furthermore, she fulfilled the roles of a wife and a mother to two children. Elizabeth Friedman was part of a team before World War II. She and her spouse, William Friedman (credited with coining the word "cryptanalysis"), devised innovative techniques for deciphering codes, documented in a series of eight booklets, that laid the groundwork for the contemporary field of cryptology. Both Elizebeth and William who would later become her husband made significant contributions to the prosecution of both world wars. However, Elizebeth's work was often kept secret, and her numerous achievements remained unknown until recently. In contrast, William received recognition, was hailed as the "world's greatest cryptologist," and was regarded as the "father of the National Security Agency."

An Aptitude for Deciphering

Clara Elizabeth Smith, the last-born among a total of nine siblings, was born on August 26, 1892 and brought up in a Quaker household in Indiana, characterized by a working-class background. Her father, John Marion Smith, was a Republican politician and Civil War hero. He could trace his lineage back to an ancestor who had immigrated on the same ship as William Penn, the influential English Quaker leader, who played a crucial role in establishing the American Commonwealth of Pennsylvania. This region was intended to serve as a safe haven for Quakers and other religious minorities from Europe, promoting religious freedom. In order to prevent her kid from being called "Eliza," Sopha Smith deliberately chose an unconventional spelling for her daughter's name.

Elizebeth received her education from local schools in Huntington. Despite her father's objections, she sent applications to other institutions. However, upon receiving acceptance to the College of Wooster in Ohio, her father provided her with a loan for tuition, charging an interest rate of 6 percent. She enrolled in Hillsdale College in Michigan and pursued a degree in English literature and a minor in the applied sciences. Additionally, she dedicated time to studying Latin, Greek, and German. She had a preference for the works of William Shakespeare and Alfred, Lord Tennyson. After graduating in 1915, she worked as a teacher and principal at a rural school for a year before becoming eager for more excitement.

In the summer of 1916, she journeyed to Chicago. During her visit to the Newberry Library in pursuit of employment, she unexpectedly encountered authentic folios of Shakespeare's works, which sparked her resolve to delve into the study of the renowned playwright. The librarian introduced her to George Fabyan, a wealthy and eccentric textile mogul who ran Riverbank Laboratories, which might be considered a think tank in Geneva, Illinois. Fabyan, who firmly believed that Sir Francis Bacon was the actual writer of Shakespeare's plays and sonnets, enlisted Elizebeth to assist him in uncovering concealed Baconian codes within Shakespeare's literary works.

The librarian who conducted the interview with Mrs. Friedman on her initial day is acknowledged for initiating a telephone conversation with Colonel

Fabyan that would profoundly alter the life of the individual known as Miss Smith at that time. During her telephone talk, the librarian expressed Smith's fondness for Shakespeare, along with other interests. Colonel Fabyan, a prosperous textile merchant, promptly encountered Miss Smith, and they deliberated over the prospective lifestyle at Riverbank, Fabyan's expansive estate situated in Geneva, Illinois. He informed Miss Smith that she would aid Elizabeth Wells Gallup, a woman from Boston, and her sister in their endeavor to establish that Sir Francis Bacon was the true author of Shakespeare's plays and sonnets. This would be accomplished by decoding a hidden message believed to be present within the works.

Elizebeth acquired her expertise in codebreaking at Riverbank, under the tutelage of Elizabeth Wells Gallup. Gallup, who oversaw the cipher school on campus, had previously authored a book in 1899 on the Bilateral Cipher of Francis Bacon. The crew at Riverbank consisted of typists, interpreters, a graduate student in genetics, and experts with expertise in acoustical engineering. Riverbank was among the pioneering establishments to advocate for the study of cryptology and other related disciplines. Prior to the establishment of the Army's Cipher Bureau, the Riverbank facility was the sole institution with the capacity to exploit and decipher encoded messages.

CHAPTER FOUR

Love and Code Breaking at Riverbank

Elizebeth Smith, 23, encountered William F. Friedman, 24, a plant geneticist and Mrs. Gallup's photo assistant, during their time at Riverbank. They were brought together due to their shared aversion towards their task, as they concluded that Mrs. Gallup was perceiving patterns that were non-existent, and a developing intrigue with codes and ciphers. William had a tendency to view ciphers as a mysterious form of entertainment, combining them with botany to create humorous and artistic expressions. William Friedman, who Miss Smith would marry in May 1917, was one of the fifteen staff members at Riverbank.

William went to the United States with his family when he was a very young child. He pursued a degree in genetics at Cornell University, which he completed in 1914. Elizebeth Smith obtained a Bachelor of Arts degree in English from Hillsdale College in Michigan in the year 1915. They crossed paths at the Riverbank Laboratories in Geneva, Illinois, where they eventually immersed themselves in the field of cryptology, frequently collaborating with the government to decipher diplomatic letters. During 1917-1918, William was enlisted in the U.S. Army and was stationed in France where he conducted analysis on German code books. The newly married couple collaborated for around four years in the only cryptologic laboratory in the country during that period. Mr. and Mrs. Friedman relocated to Washington, DC in 1921 to serve in the employment of the War Department.

Deciphering the Zimmermann Telegram at Riverbank

On March 1, 1917, the American populace became aware of a German proposition to form an alliance with Mexico in the event that the United States joined the war. Prior to the current time period, British intelligence had intercepted a confidential communication from German Foreign Minister Arthur Zimmermann to the Mexican government. In this message, Zimmermann proposed a partnership between Germany, Mexico, and Japan with the aim of regaining the southwestern states that Mexico had lost to the United States during the Mexican War of 1846-47. The message disclosed intentions to recommence unregulated submarine warfare and establish a coalition with Mexico and Japan in the event of the United States declaring war on Germany. The British intercepted the communication and then transmitted it to the United States. The release of the message sparked widespread anger and played a role in the United States' decision to participate in World War I.

The British interception was initiated years in advance. In 1914, when war was about to break out, the British promptly sent a ship to sever Germany's five trans-Atlantic cables and six underwater cables connecting Britain and Germany. Shortly after the commencement of the war, the British adeptly intercepted the international cable lines that Germany had borrowed from neutral nations to transmit their communications. Britain commenced the acquisition of substantial quantities of intelligence communications.

Amidst World War I, Riverbank Laboratories underwent a metamorphosis into a breeding ground for American cryptographic operations. Elizabeth and William assumed the responsibility as the leading couple in the initial significant cryptanalytic endeavor of the U.S. military. On 16 January 1917, Arthur Zimmermann, the foreign minister of Germany, dispatched the telegram to Mexico. Mexico was offered an alliance to jointly wage war against the United States in exchange for the restoration of its lost territories in Texas, New Mexico, and Arizona.

The Zimmermann Telegram, transmitted in cipher, altered the course of life for the Friedmans, who held expertise that became highly prized by the U.S. government. The military was in dire need of cryptanalysts, and advancements in radio and wireless technology were altering the dynamics of warfare. There were maybe only three or four individuals in the entire United States who possessed the ability to decipher codes, and Elizebeth and William were among this exclusive group. Elizebeth was the first individual to decipher military communications received from the Mexican Army, employing a method of analyzing the frequency of letters.

The Friedmans commenced functioning as a cohesive unit, formulating strategies in an improvisational manner. During the initial eight months of the war, they and their limited team were responsible for all codebreaking operations across several branches of the U.S. government, while also devising enduring approaches that are still employed today. Both individuals lacked proficiency in arithmetic, nevertheless they relied on their intuitive abilities to develop strategies for identifying patterns. A crucial aspect was the scientific nature of their techniques, ensuring that the outcomes could be reproduced. The Friedmans diligently sought to decipher incoming signals. The intercepted texts from Scotland Yard unveiled a complex separatist scheme orchestrated by Hindu activists residing in New York, aimed at transporting weapons to India with the assistance of Germany. William was called upon to provide testimony regarding his method of deciphering the codes. However, before he had the opportunity to testify, an Indian man in the audience fired a gunshot at one of the defendants.

Meanwhile, Fabyan proposed Riverbank as a school for codebreaking, attracting 80 young cops who applied along with their spouses. Elizebeth and William exemplified the effectiveness of a spousal partnership.

CHAPTER FIVE

Mission Outsmart the Rum Syndicates and the Prohibition Era

During World War II when the renowned intelligence officer William J. "Wild Bill" Donovan created a cryptographic division, he selected Elizebeth Friedman to initiate and manage the project, recognizing her as an indispensable asset. Friedman and her colleagues utilized the Hagelin cipher machine to diligently work day and night, successfully generating the necessary code systems in a matter of weeks.

In 1921, both Friedmans commenced employment with the government, with William joining the Army Reserve Signal Corps and Elizebeth assuming a civilian role. She tendered her resignation after one year in order to pursue writing and establish a family. William became a part of the immediate and important endeavor to develop cipher machines, which resulted in an increase in his renown.

In 1925, the Treasury Department's Coast Guard sought Elizebeth's participation in its newly established Intelligence Division, with the aim of intercepting rumrunners. The Coast

Guard required expedited development of codebreaking proficiency while also safeguarding its own communications from the astute criminals who were monitoring governmental transmissions intended for ships and agents. The Coast Guard had been intercepting signals from multiple radio towers along the East Coast that were utilized for search-and-rescue operations. However, they faced a backlog of intercepted messages that were still to be decoded due to a lack of personnel available for the task. Elizebeth successfully deciphered over 650 messages in 24 distinct cryptographic schemes employed by illicit organizations operating throughout the Texas Gulf Coast.

The Coast Guard cutter Dexter sank the notorious Canadian rumrunning vessel, the I'm Alone, in 1929. Canada lodged an official objection and requested $400,000 restitution, contending that according to a 1924 treaty, the United States had committed to refraining from inspecting and confiscating ships that were more than an hour's sailing distance away from U.S. coasts, unless the chase originated in U.S. territorial waters. The Coast Guard endeavored to establish documentary evidence that the vessel named I'm Alone was present within the territorial waters of the United States at the time of its initial encounter. Elizebeth's decipherments aided federal authorities in substantiating that the vessel named "I'm Alone" was, in fact, originally located within territorial waters and was a clandestine ship used for smuggling alcohol, owned by American criminals. Her work received acclaim from both Canada and the United States.

Coast Guard Commandant Frederick C. Billard was greatly pleased by the significant role cryptology played in proving the innocence of the United States in the I'm Alone case. As a result, he presented Elizebeth's proposal for an improved cryptology unit to Congress in 1930, seeking funds. At that time, Elizebeth Friedman had successfully deciphered 12,000 letters related to illegal alcohol transportation in the past three years, with the assistance of only one female clerk.

In 1931, she was appointed as the head cryptologist of CG Unit 387, with an annual pay of $3,800. Her team commenced deciphering codes for each of the six Treasury agencies. The efforts of the Coast Guard in cryptanalysis and radio intelligence during Prohibition proved to be fruitful while facing national security challenges in World War II.

The period of Prohibition in the United States, from 1920 to 1933, involved the legal prohibition on the production, sale, and transit of alcoholic drinks, as mandated by the Eighteenth Amendment. In spite of the broad backing for the temperance movement, which effectively brought about the passing of this law, a significant number of Americans were willing to partake in the consumption of distilled spirits in violation of the law. This led to the rise of bootlegging (the illegal production and sale of liquor) and speakeasies (secret drinking establishments), both of which were taken advantage of by organized crime. Therefore, the Prohibition era is widely known as a period defined by gangsterism, where intense competition and violent territorial disputes were prevalent among criminal syndicates.

Elizebeth's activities during the Prohibition era garnered her widespread attention in the media, turning her into a sensation. Although she gained public prominence, William's military activities remained confidential. He established a squad called the Signal Intelligence Service with the purpose of deciphering the Japanese diplomatic code. He invented the SIGABA, a sophisticated encryption device equipped with 15 rotors. A total of 10,060 devices would be supplied to all theaters of World War II. William concealed this task from Elizebeth, not divulging any information about it.

Following the lifting of Prohibition in 1934, rumrunners transitioned to illicitly transporting heroin and morphine. Elizebeth transitioned to deciphering communications among drug traffickers. In 1938, the Royal

Canadian Mounted Police transported her by air to Vancouver in order to examine communications found on a Chinese merchant's premises. Utilizing a Chinese dictionary, she successfully deciphered the messages and uncovered a clandestine operation involved in the illicit trade of Canadian weaponry to Hong Kong in exchange for narcotics. All five offenders were convicted as a result of her evidence. Simultaneously, she successfully pursued a master's degree in archaeology at an American University.

CHAPTER SIX

The Greatest Spy Roundup

During the period from 1938 to 1941, the Treasury Department's responsibilities were extended to include the enforcement of neutrality, in addition to its existing law enforcement tasks, as the threat of war loomed. In 1940, Elizebeth, while deciphering intercepted communications that she initially believed to be related to smuggling, noticed a change and determined that the messages were actually in German. These messages were being transmitted from unidentified radio stations located in Mexico, South America, and the United States. The content of these messages included classified details about the shipping routes of the United States and Britain, as well as information about the production capabilities of American factories. When two stations exchange signals, they form a "circuit" that is safeguarded by an individual code that must be deciphered. Elizebeth had to maintain complete invisibility while accessing the circuits. The cryptanalytic unit she led started engaging in counterespionage and counterintelligence activities, which were so confidential that their classification would be maintained for many years.

In 1941, J. Edgar Hoover, the Director of the FBI, requested Elizebeth and her team from the Coast Guard to provide training to FBI agents who were going to be assigned to South America. However, Hoover quickly claimed full credit when they successfully decrypted messages exchanged between Nazi agents in New York and Latin America. He referred to this achievement as the "greatest spy roundup" in the history of the United States. The Germans residing in Hamburg had made a formal request to the Nazi operative stationed on Long

Island to transmit communications from Mexico. This was because the covert station in Mexico did not possess a transmitter of sufficient strength to establish communication with Germany. Elizebeth Friedman was establishing a strong reputation as a skilled problem solver. She transitioned into a role where she moved from one agency to another, assisting each in the development of their individual cryptographic services.

Asset Owned by Wild Bill

In the same year, COI Director Donovan made a request to Friedman to create a cryptology office for his new organization and develop a secure communications network. Various intelligence services were vying for the most skilled cryptographers, radio operators, and equipment. Donovan frequently sought resources from other government organizations. However, despite his significant power, he was unable to seize assets from two of the nation's greatest crypto-communications agencies: Army SIS and Navy OP-20-G. He chose an agency with a communications group that was too small to protect itself from being recruited by others. In November 1941, the Secretary of the Treasury agreed to Donovan's request that the Coast Guard's code and cipher branch redirect its efforts towards creating a functional cryptographic unit for his communication network.

Donovan had been relying on the State Department for his international communication. However, he desired to have his own distinct cryptography equipment, codes, and trained personnel. Friedman and her team gathered the essential equipment, including secure envelopes for confidential messages, cross-section paper for encoding and decoding, and frames utilized in strip-cipher code systems. She acquired two Hagelin cipher machines intended for other agencies. The Hagelin, referred to as the "lug and pin," was a portable device capable of both encryption and printing. Donovan desired to have the unit operational within an unreasonably brief timeframe, prompting Elizabeth and her team to labor continuously. In only a matter of weeks, they successfully developed tailored coding systems, such as double transpositions and strip ciphers, specifically designed for COI activities. She utilized her connections inside the intelligence community to get two highly coveted automatic encryption machines. Subsequently, she dedicated a significant portion of December to the process of encoding and decoding the initial messages of COI.

Donovan regarded her presence at COI as extremely valuable and made efforts to permanently transfer her to his group. Nevertheless, in late December, she resumed her duties in the Coast Guard, while Lieutenant Leonard T. Jones, another member of the Coast Guard, took up the duty for COI's newly established cryptographic section. Prior to her departure, she composed a scathing letter addressed to Donovan, conveyed through his intermediary, Marine Captain James Roosevelt. In the letter, she meticulously outlined all her achievements on his behalf within a brief span of two months, while also providing him with precise recommendations. He appropriated all of them. The War Report of the OSS described Friedman's message center as the sole communications function that was adequately established during COI.

CHAPTER SEVEN

Connection Between Argentina and Nazi Germany

After completing her assignment for Donovan, Friedman and her Coast Guard Unit 387 commenced intercepting and deciphering the communications of enemy spies in the Western Hemisphere by the second month of the war. The Coast Guard deployed radiomen throughout Brazil to intercept radio communications transmitted by German spies. Friedman decrypted intercepted messages sent to the Abwehr, the German military intelligence agency, which indicated that the operatives were seeking information about American companies involved in the processing of uranium ore. She exerted effort to decipher signals including information about the paths of Allied vessels and transmit the decrypted messages to the military before U-boat captains could access the information. By the end of the first quarter of 1942, U-boats had successfully destroyed one million tons of commerce and caused the deaths of 5,000 seamen from the Allied forces. Adolf Hitler offered a reward for the destruction of the troopship RMS Queen

Mary. The decrypts provided by Friedman were received by the captain in a timely manner, enabling him to execute evasive maneuvers and ultimately saving almost 8,000 lives. Collaborating with a team of less than 20 individuals, she devised a complex plan to join a coalition of South American nations that were loyal to Germany. Additionally, she orchestrated covert transactions for the exchange of weaponry between Argentina and Germany. Her decryption efforts uncovered a well-organized group of individuals planning a fascist coup and exposing the intricate network of Nazi spies operating in South America. These decrypts were classified as ULTRA. They presented evidence of Argentina's collaboration with Nazi Germany, enabling the Allies to exert diplomatic pressure on the Argentine government to completely cut ties with Berlin. The deciphering of German codes enabled the Allies to effectively eliminate numerous Abwehr missions in the Western Hemisphere.

Friedman's Later Life and Death

Since Friedman held a civilian position, Coast Guard Lieutenant Commander Leonard T. Jones, whom she had instructed, assumed the role of her superior. Jones received all the recognition as her name was never included in official memos. Scholars were alerted years later following the declassification of Coast Guard decrypts by the presence of only her initials, "ESF," at the bottom. It is evident from historical records that Friedman played a crucial role in World War II by identifying and neutralizing a worldwide network of covert Nazis. She accomplished this by deciphering 4,000 written messages and gaining expertise in operating 48 secret radio channels and three Enigma machines. She successfully thwarted coup attempts and created divisions between Germany and her allies.

Lieutenant Commander Jones was honored with multiple accolades for the wartime efforts of Unit 387, including the prestigious Legion of Merit, the World War II Victory Medal, the National Defense Service Medal, the Navy Unit Commendation Ribbon, and the Order of the British Empire. Elizebeth Friedman's salary increased from $4,200 to $5,390, resulting in a higher payment.

In her Christmas letter of 1944, she stated that her husband had received the Exceptional Service Award with Gold Wreath, while she had been doing the responsibilities of a "routine navy job." William received several prestigious awards for his covert contributions throughout the war, including the War Department medal for outstanding Civilian Service, the Presidential Medal for Merit, and the Presidential National Security Medal. Following the conclusion of World War II, the government consolidated cryptography operations from other agencies and reduced Elizebeth's role in codebreaking inside the Coast Guard. She transitioned to the International Monetary Fund (IMF), where she served as a "Consultant in Communications" from 1946 until 1949. The information regarding her job at that place is vague, however, brief allusions in her documents indicate that she maintained her discreet position as a "fixer," assisting the IMF in ensuring the security and preservation of its communication tools. Elizebeth Friedman passed away in a nursing home in New Jersey on October 31,

1980, without ever disclosing the specifics of her wartime efforts, just alluding to them as "spy-related matters." Her codebreaking work during World War II was not acknowledged in any of her obituaries. The historical records of Unit 387 were kept confidential for a period of 62 years, until 2008.

During the final years of her life, she dedicated her time to collating her and her husband's documents and commencing her memoirs. She is well recognized among cryptographers as a legendary figure in their industry.

While collaborating closely with her husband William as a team, Mrs. Friedman made numerous distinct contributions to the field of cryptology. She successfully decrypted numerous encoded letters during the Prohibition era and independently resolved several prominent cases, including codes written in Mandarin Chinese. It has been established that the complexity or difficulty was irrelevant. Elizebeth Smith Friedman, who had been in her industry for almost fifty years, had undeniably established herself as a trailblazer in the field of code breaking.

END